Football School

Name: ....

Class: ....

Coaches: ....

Kickito Ergo Sum

I celebrated
World Book Day 2021
with this gift from my local
bookseller and Walker Books
#ShareAStory

First published 2021 by Walker Books Ltd
87 Vauxhall Walk, London SE11 5HJ

2 4 6 8 10 9 7 5 3 1

Text © 2021 Alex Bellos and Ben Lyttleton
Illustrations © 2021 Spike Gerrell

The right of Alex Bellos and Ben Lyttleton, and Spike Gerrell
to be identified as authors and illustrator respectively of this work
has been asserted by them in accordance with the Copyright,
Designs and Patents Act 1988

This book has been typeset in Gill Sans MT Pro and WB Spike

Printed and bound in Germany by GGP Media GmbH

British Library Cataloguing in Publication Data:
a catalogue record for this book is available from the British Library

ISBN 978-1-5295-0050-9

WALKER
BOOKS

FSC
www.fsc.org
MIX
Paper from
responsible sources
FSC® C020471

www.walker.co.uk
www.footballschool.co

FOOTBALL SCHOOL

★ 20 ★
≡ FANTASTIC ≡

FOOTBALL STORIES

FULL OF AWESOME FACTS ABOUT FOOTBALL AND THE WORLD!

Alex Bellos & Ben Lyttleton

Illustrated by Spike Gerrell

Welcome to Football School 20 Fantastic Football Stories!
World Book Day edition!
I'm Alex!
And I'm Ben!
We're your teachers.
We mean coaches!
We think the WORLD of football.
So we've put our favourite stories in this BOOK.
Which will have you in a DAZE!
You will get to read all about some amazing players.
Like the youngest player to score in the Champions League.
And the striker who helped feed millions of children.
I'm hungry to know more!
Seconds, anyone?
AB
BL

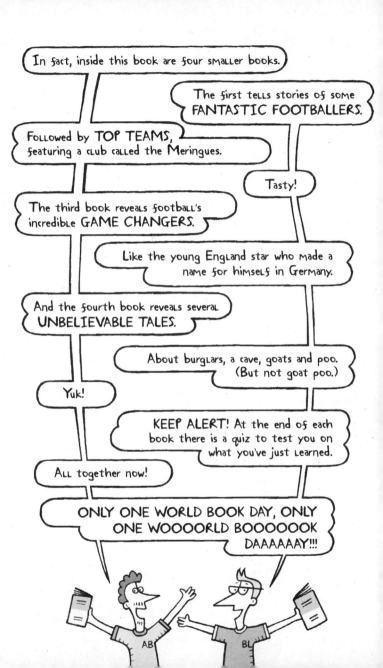

CONTENTS

FANTASTIC FOOTBALLERS

Ansu Fati	10
Harry Kane	14
Megan Rapinoe	18
Marcus Rashford	22
Cristiano Ronaldo	24
Fantastic Footballers Quiz	28

TOP TEAMS

England Women	30
Forest Green Rovers	32
Leicester City	36
Liverpool	40
Real Madrid	44
Top Teams Quiz	48

GAME CHANGERS

Dick, Kerr's Ladies	50
Jimmy Hill	54
Craig Johnston	56
Jadon Sancho	60
Walter Tull	64
Game Changers Quiz	68

UNBELIEVABLE TALES

The Boy Who Would Not Grow	70
The Footballers Who Pooed on the Pitch	74
The GOAT Mascot	78
The Mystery of the Stolen World Cup	80
The Thai Cave Rescue	84
Unbelievable Tales Quiz	88
Quiz Answers	89

WORLD BOOK DAY

World Book Day's mission is to offer every child and young person the opportunity to read and love books by giving you the chance to have a book of your own.

To find out more, and for loads of fun activities and recommendations to help you keep reading, visit worldbookday.com

World Book Day is a charity funded by publishers and booksellers in the UK and Ireland.

World Book Day is also made possible by generous sponsorship from National Book Tokens and support from authors and illustrators.

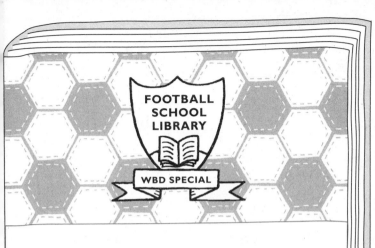

FANTASTIC
FOOTBALLERS

A. BELLOS
&
B. LYTTLETON

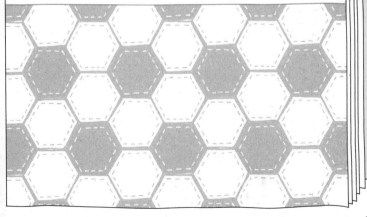

ANSU FATI

Born: 2002
Country: Spain
Position: Left-winger

Ansu Fati is a record-breaking winger with the world at his feet: he is the youngest player ever to score a league goal for Barcelona, the youngest player to score for Spain and the youngest player to score in the Champions League. He managed all three feats before he turned eighteen!

Lionel Messi has tipped the rapid youngster to reach the top, which is just as well – Fati's emergence in the Barcelona team came when Messi was entering the swansong of his career. Fati looks set to be crowned his natural replacement.

There are similarities between the two players. Both were born outside Spain: Messi in Argentina and Fati in Guinea-Bissau in West Africa. Both moved to Barcelona's youth academy, La Masia, at a young age: Messi at thirteen and Fati, after turning down Real Madrid, at ten. And both have exceptional skills and an eye for goal. Fati may even be the faster of the two!

Fati took his chance in the Barcelona team in 2019, after a spate of injuries hit Messi and Barcelona's other strikers, Luis Suárez and Ousmane Dembélé. He was just sixteen years old when he came off the bench to head home a goal in only his second appearance. That made him the youngest player ever to score for the club – even Messi waited until he was nearly eighteen for his first Barcelona goal! When Fati started a match soon after, he scored within two minutes. This teenager was in a hurry to the top!

Spain's national team was keen to select Fati, who also qualified to play for his birth country, Guinea-Bissau, and for Portugal. It did not take long to see why Spain wanted him. In his second match, Fati won a penalty after 90 seconds, and later curled in a shot that went in off the post. Another game, another goal, and another record smashed!

Fati normally plays on the left wing and likes to cut inside and shoot with his right foot. His pace makes him almost impossible to tackle. He has also impressed observers with his movement off the ball, and with his ability to cope with the pressure and attention from fans and the media. Nothing seems to phase Fati.

Barcelona was so determined to keep Fati that they gave him a new contract the following season, and placed his value at an eye-watering £425 million. "I hope I can be at Barcelona all my life," Fati said.

Barcelona will be hoping for the same!

FRIENDS AND RIVALS

When he was in Barcelona's youth academy, Fati formed a devastating strike partnership with a player from Japan called Takefusa Kubo. In one season for the Under-12s, the pair scored 130 goals between them. Kubo left Barcelona but ended up back in Spain when he signed for Real Madrid. Fati and Kubo have not let their clubs' rivalry ruin their friendship. Mates before teams!

HARRY KANE

Born: 1993
Country: England
Position: Centre-forward

Relentless in training and prolific in front of goal, Harry Kane is the hard-working centre-forward who overcame a series of rejections to become England captain and the Golden Boot winner for scoring the most goals at the 2018 World Cup. Humble Harry is a true hero!

Kane started out at Arsenal's academy, but he was released when he was eight. "We'll just work harder and find another club," his dad told him. That's exactly what Kane did – although it took time. Kane was eleven when he joined the Tottenham Hotspur academy. At eighteen, he was sent on loan to clubs playing in lower divisions, like Leyton

Orient, Millwall, Norwich and Leicester City. He scored a handful of goals but never stood out as a star of the future. Kane wondered if he'd ever play in the Premier League. He later said that coming through these episodes of self-doubt, and developing resilience in the face of adversity, was crucial to his career success.

He was stuck on the substitutes' bench at Leicester when he watched an American football documentary that changed his mindset. Kane learned that the New England Patriots quarterback, Tom Brady, was always overlooked as a youngster. Brady worked obsessively to improve and became one of the most successful players in American football history. Kane was inspired: he even called one of his dogs Brady! From that day on, he was going to be like Brady and work as hard as possible to get his chance.

His moment came in November 2014 when, after scoring a few goals for Spurs in cup competitions, he scored his first Premier League goal with a last-minute free kick to beat Aston Villa. "All the things I went through before I scored Goal Number One … that's what made me who I am," he said. Kane kept his place in the team and went on to score over 30 goals that season. A Spurs star was born.

Kane never stopped scoring: in November 2020, he scored goal number 200 for Spurs. With over 150 Premier League goals, he is closing in on Alan Shearer's record as the league's all-time leading scorer. As Kane developed, it turned out that he was good at everything – scoring with either foot, holding up the ball, crossing for team-mates and heading. His main strength, though, was his drive and determination: the continued effort he put in to improve his game. He stayed late after training for extra shooting, focusing on aiming low in the corners. He became stronger and faster, took ice baths to aid his recovery, employed a chef at home to ensure his nutrition was correct and even learned to love eating fish. His dedication extended to his fans: he once spent two hours in the stadium car park signing autographs.

STAR SCHOOL

Harry Kane went to the same school as former England star David Beckham. This is just one of the things they have in common. Both footballers have also captained the England national team.

These are the reasons why England coach Gareth Southgate appointed him captain before the 2018 World Cup. "He is absolutely the role model you want," said Southgate. England reached the World Cup semi-final and Kane was the top scorer in the tournament with six goals, becoming only the second Englishman (after Gary Lineker in 1986) to win the Golden Boot.

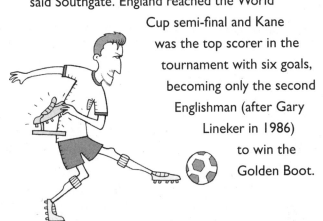

MEGAN RAPINOE

Born: 1985
Country: USA
Position: Winger

Megan **R**apinoe dyed her hair bright pink for the 2019 World Cup, but that was only one of the reasons the USA winger stood out. Rapinoe was a well-known campaigner for equality and tolerance as well as a key part of the USA team that had won the previous World Cup. She was the USA captain in 2019, and the team was tipped to win the title again.

Halfway through the tournament Rapinoe became its most talked-about player. She had a public row with the most powerful person in the world, Donald Trump, who at that time was the president of the USA.

In the USA, when the national football team wins the World Cup, it is traditional for them to pay a visit to the president at his residence, the White House. But Rapinoe said that if her team won she would refuse to go. She said her refusal was because she disagreed with President Trump's attitude towards women and Black people.

It isn't the first time that Rapinoe has spoken up for her beliefs. She is as fearless in standing up for her principles as she is at tormenting defenders on the pitch. She has criticized her bosses at US Soccer for wage discrimination, and she and her girlfriend, a professional basketball player, were the first gay couple to appear on the cover of an American sports magazine.

However, Rapinoe had not made controversial comments so openly, or at such a crucial time for the team, as those directed against President Trump.

When President Trump heard about her comments he was furious. He said she should go and win the tournament before speaking out.

SISTER SLOGANS

Rapinoe has set up a fashion label with her twin sister Rachael. Their slogan is Be Your Best You – which is appropriate, as this Megan is the best Megan we know!

He warned her not to disrespect her own country. Never before has the leader of a country had such a public falling out with the biggest star in its national team.

The pressure on Rapinoe was enormous going into the quarter-final against hosts France. But it took just five minutes for her to make her mark, with a smart goal from a free kick outside the area. She ran to the touchline with her team-mates behind her, and faced the cheering crowd with her arms spread wide, and chest out. The goal celebration made her look defiant and proud, and it became known as The Pose.

Rapinoe scored again in the second half; it was the crucial winning goal as

France netted a late consolation. Rapinoe was injured for the semi-final match against England, which the USA won 2–1, but she was fit again for the final. And she was back on the scoresheet too, opening the scoring with a neat penalty in USA's 2–0 win over the Netherlands.

USA were the winners of the 2019 World Cup. Rapinoe scooped the Golden Boot for top goal-scorer. Later that year she also won the Ballon D'Or for the world's best player.

Rapinoe's triumphs in 2019 were especially sweet because she had also silenced her most high-profile critic, President Trump.

And did she – or the team – visit President Trump at the White House? What do you think? Of course not! Megan Rapinoe is a star who sticks fiercely to her principles.

MARCUS RASHFORD

Born: 1997
Country: England
Position: Forward

England striker
Marcus Rashford spent his time during the coronavirus pandemic doing something far more important than scoring goals. He persuaded the British government to help hungry children receive free meals.

There are over one million children in England who rely on eating some of their meals at school every day. Rashford was one of them not so long ago. He grew up in Manchester with his mum and four siblings. Rashford went to a breakfast club in the morning, had a free school lunch, then an after-school snack, before his mum would cook dinner for the family after coming in late from work.

Rashford went on to become centre-forward for his local team, Manchester United, and then a regular starter for England. As his fame grew, so did his determination to help the next generation of vulnerable children. During the pandemic, he worked with a food charity to raise funds to deliver food to hungry children when schools were closed.

He led a campaign to ensure children received free school meals in all holidays during the pandemic. He personally persuaded Prime Minister Boris Johnson to promise that the government would spend over £400 million to support children in need. "Can we not all agree that no child should be going to bed hungry?" Rashford said.

In October 2020, Rashford was recognized by the Queen as an MBE (Member of the Order of the British Empire) for his efforts in fighting child food poverty. Rashford has shown the world that he is a hero both on and off the pitch.

CRISTIANO RONALDO

Born: 1985
Country: Portugal
Position: Centre-forward

Cristiano Ronaldo has won league titles and Champions League finals. He has broken goal-scoring records and lifted the Ballon D'Or. But his most memorable game is one in which he did not score a dramatic winner or bag a hat-trick. It was the 2016 Euro final, in which Portugal was up against France. The game would become known as The Ronaldo Final – but not for the reasons you might expect.

Portugal had never won an international tournament and Ronaldo was desperate to win. At the 2016 Euros, Portugal were a defensively solid team that relied on Ronaldo's individual brilliance. He was captain and had played a huge role in helping Portugal reach the final.

In the knockout matches, Ronaldo was decisive: he set up Portugal's winner against Croatia, then scored in the penalty shoot-out win over Poland. His goal and assist in the semi-final against Wales clinched Portugal's spot in the final. Their opponents were France, the tournament hosts who, with the likes of Paul Pogba and Antoine Griezmann, were expected to win.

Seven minutes into the final, Ronaldo collided with France winger Dimitri Payet and fell to the ground clutching his knee. The whole of Portugal held its breath. He received treatment and limped back onto the pitch. He could barely walk and with tears in his eyes, he asked the coach to replace him.

The star player was stretchered off with not even half an hour of the match played. Every Portuguese fan's greatest nightmare had come true; on the biggest stage of all, Ronaldo would not be able to save the day for his nation. Surely Portugal's chances were ruined.

Ronaldo watched the rest of the game, which finished 0–0, from the sidelines.

In the period before extra time, he walked around each of his team-mates, urging them to make one last effort towards making history.

As the last 30 minutes of the match played out, Ronaldo became even more animated. He stood next to coach Fernando Santos, limping heavily as he bellowed out tactical instructions. Ronaldo was demonstrating the desire to win that has pushed him to become one of the best players of his generation.

The game was decided ten minutes before the end. One of Portugal's substitutes, Eder, hit a low shot from outside the area that whizzed into the corner of the France net. Ronaldo could not have done it better himself!

On the sideline, Ronaldo pumped his fists in excitement. When the final whistle blew, confirming Portugal as European champions, Ronaldo cried again, though this time the tears were of relief, joy and happiness. Ronaldo had dragged Portugal to the final, and his team-mates repaid him in the best way possible.

Ronaldo had broken several individual records during the tournament – including all-time top goal-scorer and appearance-maker, as well as the only player to score in four different tournaments – but winning the final as a team was the only thing that mattered to him. He tied a Portugal flag around his waist and hobbled towards the presentation area to lift the trophy. With tears in his eyes, he hoisted aloft the trophy. One of the greatest individual players in the game had helped his country make history.

QUIZ

1. **Ansu Fati plays for Spain but in what African country was he born?**

   a) Senegal
   b) The Gambia
   c) Mali
   d) Guinea-Bissau

2. **Harry Kane went to the same school as which previous England captain?**

   a) Wayne Rooney
   b) David Beckham
   c) Bobby Moore
   d) Steven Gerrard

3. **Why was Marcus Rashford awarded an MBE in 2020?**

   a) For his superb football skills
   b) For his efforts in fighting child food poverty
   c) He rescued a cat from a tree.
   d) He donated money to charity.

4. **Which high-profile critic did Megan Rapinoe silence by helping USA win the 2019 World Cup?**

   a) Boris Johnson
   b) Her mum
   c) President Trump
   d) Lady Gaga

5. **How did Cristiano Ronaldo help Portugal win the 2016 Euro final?**

   a) He coached the team from the sidelines.
   b) He picked the team.
   c) He scored a hat-trick.
   d) He saved a penalty.

FOOTBALL SCHOOL LIBRARY

TOP **TEAMS**

WBD SPECIAL

A. BELLOS & B. LYTTLETON

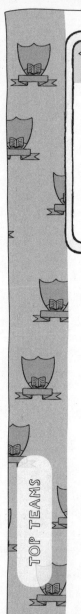
☆☆☆ England Women ☆

Country: England
Nickname:
The Lionesses
National stadium:
Wembley

England women's team cemented their status as one of the world's best teams by reaching two World Cup semi-finals in the last two tournaments. Both matches saw unpredictable twists that have made the brave Lionesses even more popular!

At the 2015 World Cup, the Lionesses faced a semi-final against Japan. The score was 1–1 with less than one minute to play when defender Laura Bassett, trying to cut out a cross, somehow flicked the ball from distance into her own net. The injury-time own goal knocked England out. Bassett said she was heartbroken. The team had so narrowly missed out on a place in the final.

In the 2019 World Cup, England won four straight matches to earn a semi-final against reigning champions USA. Could this be the moment they finally reached the World Cup final? Bassett, now retired from football and watching from the stands, was hoping it would be.

USA took an early lead before Ellen White levelled the scores. There was still hope. Alex Morgan put USA ahead again, and celebrated by pretending to drink a cup of English tea. The Lionesses pushed forward: White had a goal disallowed before England were awarded a penalty with a few minutes left to play.

Steph Houghton, the captain, stepped up to take the spot kick. This was England's big chance. The country held its breath ... but her kick lacked power and USA's goalkeeper saved it. USA held on to win. After the game, Houghton said she was heartbroken – the same word Bassett had used four years earlier.

The Lionesses are still waiting to reach the World Cup final. But they are getting closer every time!

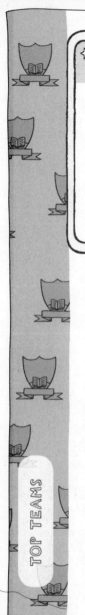

☆☆☆ Forest Green Rovers ☆

Country: England
Nickname:
The Green Devils
Stadium:
The New Lawn

Forest Green Rovers are a team that are changing the world. Located in Nailsworth, a small town in the Gloucestershire countryside, the club has played in League Two, England's fourth tier, since 2017. As well as winning matches, Forest Green Rovers want to show that football can play its part in helping to save the planet.

The club is helping to protect the planet by recycling, not using harmful chemicals and using renewable resources, such as sunlight and rainwater. Often people use the word "green" to describe these types of environmentally friendly activities. FIFA has called Forest Green the greenest club in the world! Let's take a look at what they are doing differently.

Saving water

Forest Green Rovers collect their own rainwater. Some is saved from the stadium roof and some from drains below the pitch, which flow into a water tank. When full, the tank can hold enough water to fill over 600 bathtubs! Their aim is to collect enough rainwater for free so that their grounds team can water the pitch using the club's own reserves without ever switching on the tap.

Banning chemicals

To get perfect luscious green grass on the pitch, most grounds teams will use fertilizers and pesticides. But these often contain chemicals that are harmful to humans and animals, including insects such as bees. At Forest Green, the grounds team don't use pesticides and they only use fertilizers that are safe for humans and animals.

Using the sun

Our electricity often comes from burning fossil fuels, such as coal, in power stations. Fossil fuels are a non-renewable source of energy, which means that one day they will run out. But electricity can be made from renewable sources, which means that they can be used again and again. One example is the sun. A solar panel absorbs sunlight and turns it into electricity. The Forest Green stadium has 170 solar panels on its roof, which provide the club with free electricity that creates no pollution.

Reducing pollution

Forest Green Rovers are trying to reduce their use of fossil fuels on the pitch too. They have a solar-powered robot lawnmower that mows by itself. It takes three days to mow the whole pitch and it will text the grounds team if it gets into trouble. We hope it uses an e-mow-ji!

TOP TEAMS

Eating green

The meat industry is having a negative impact on the planet, because farming animals uses up lots of resources, including land, food and water. Forest Green Rovers believe it is better to eat a vegetarian diet, which means not eating meat products in favour of options made from plants instead. Hungry fans at their stadium are offered a Q-Pie, which is made from Quorn, a meat substitute created from fungus.

GREEN GOALS

Here's a checklist of things you can do to help the planet. What else can you add to the list?

- Take a reusable water bottle to matches

- Turn the TV off after *Match of the Day* – don't leave it on standby

- Do a litter pick on your pitch after a game and recycle any litter

- Walk or cycle to games instead of using a car

Leicester City

Country: England
Nickname: The Foxes
Stadium: King Power

TOP TEAMS

When Leicester City won the Premier League title in 2016, it was one of the greatest sporting shocks in history. The team had only just avoided relegation the previous year and their chances of winning the league were put at 5,000 to 1. That means if the league season were to be played out 5,000 times, they would be expected to win it only once! This surprising win shows that one of the great joys of sport is that sometimes unpredictable things can actually happen...

That season, Leicester had a small squad of older players who had been rejected and released by other clubs, and young players keen to make a mark. Their new coach Claudio Ranieri turned Leicester into a counter-attacking team, who were happy for the opposition to have the ball, but who then sprung attacks quickly when they had it. This tactic allowed them to play to the strengths of unknown winger Riyad Mahrez and striker Jamie Vardy, a recent amateur player who early in the season scored in eleven consecutive games, a Premier League record.

At the halfway point of the season, Leicester were top of the table, but no one expected them to stay there. Ranieri just told his players to enjoy themselves. He kept them motivated by taking the players out for pizza after matches in which they kept a clean sheet.

In the space of four days in February, Leicester beat Liverpool 2–0 and Manchester City 3–1. Only Arsenal and Tottenham Hotspur could catch Leicester now. Leicester's next match was against Arsenal, who won thanks to a last-minute goal. Arsenal were only two points behind Leicester in the top spot. This was the point when the Foxes were expected to fall away.

In fact, the opposite happened. Ranieri gave his players a holiday to recover from the defeat and they returned full of energy. They won six of their next seven games. Arsenal won only two of their next seven.

Now it was between Leicester and Spurs. Leicester picked up points and Spurs needed to win at Chelsea to stay in the hunt. The match was played on a Monday night. The Leicester players all went to Vardy's house to watch the game. They were supporting Chelsea. Spurs went 2–0 up before Chelsea scored. Then, with seven minutes left, Chelsea's Eden Hazard curled the ball in from the edge of the area. It was a stunning goal. The 2–2 result clinched the title for Leicester.

The players celebrated in Vardy's kitchen, cheering, dancing and crying with joy. Leicester had confounded the odds and made the most of their luck; their players avoided injuries and the bigger teams had all suffered a slump in form at the same time. Nevertheless, they certainly deserved this victory, unexpected as it was.

A PANTS RESULT

Leicester's most famous fan, Gary Lineker, had made a bet with his fellow presenters on *Match of the Day* that if Leicester won the title, he would present the show wearing only his underpants. And that's exactly what he did!

Liverpool

Country: England
Nickname: The Reds
Stadium: Anfield

Liverpool were so dominant in winning the 2019–2020 Premier League season that they were top of the table after the first game and stayed there until the end of the season. Champions from first to last!

Most of all, their coach Jürgen Klopp improved each player and made them feel part of a bigger group. He reminded them they play not just for themselves, but for their team-mates, their families, the fans and the whole community. During the coronavirus lockdown, Klopp's enthusiasm helped players and other staff members who were feeling low. Klopp and his Liverpool players also called fans to cheer them up. Klopp cares!

Klopp is seen as a brilliant motivator, but he is also very smart tactically. He changed Liverpool's tactics, but even when Liverpool's opponents knew what to expect, they still could not stop them. His tactics included:

- ⚽ **Full-backs as attackers**: Right-back Trent Alexander-Arnold was Liverpool's most creative player, setting up twelve goals. Left-back Andy Robertson was only just behind, with eleven assists.

- ⚽ **Midfielders as defenders**: When the full-backs moved up, midfielder Fabinho dropped into defence to help out.

- ⚽ **Wingers as scorers**: Liverpool played in a 4-3-3 system with Sadio Mané (eighteen goals) and Mo Salah (nineteen goals) prolific from out wide.

- ⚽ **Forwards chase and press**: Klopp's pressing game starts in attack, with centre-forward Roberto Firmino the first line of defence. He only scored one goal at home all season!

Liverpool turned their stadium Anfield into a fortress and, buoyed on by their passionate fans, did not lose at home in the league. When they came back to finish off the season the stadium was empty of fans. This made it harder for the players, but they kept their record intact.

Everyone agreed that Liverpool were worthy champions. And even though the team was not able to celebrate the success with an open-top bus parade through the city, as is traditional, Klopp made sure to thank the fans. "I couldn't be more proud of my coaching staff and of all the people in Liverpool!" he said.

TOP TEAMS

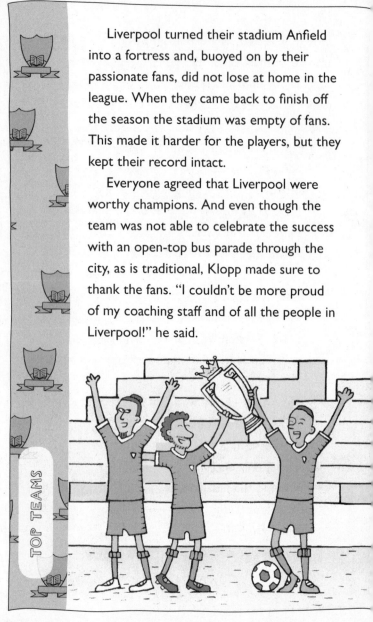

COASTING HOME

Liverpool broke the record for clinching the title with games to spare. Here are the other title-winners who were saved a stressful end to the season:

Team	Season	Games to spare
Man United	1907–08	5
Everton	1984–85	5
Man United	2000–01	5
Man City	2017–18	5
Liverpool	2019–20	7

Real Madrid

Country: Spain
Nickname:
Los Merengues
(The Meringues,
as they wear white)
Stadium:
Santiago Bernabéu

Real Madrid are the most famous club in football. Originally the team were called Madrid, but in 1920 the King of Spain allowed the club to incorporate the Spanish word *real*, meaning "royal", into their name. Football royalty indeed!

I'm keeping it real!

Real Madrid built their international reputation in the 1950s when they won the first five editions of the European Cup, the forerunner of the Champions League. Sixteen teams from across the continent took part in the first edition in 1955. The timing was perfect: shortly after the end of the Second World War, most of Europe was keen to find ways to come together after years of division.

Real Madrid beat French side Reims 4–3 in the final of the first edition. Winning the tournament guaranteed qualification the following year, and they beat Reims in the final of the second edition too. Madrid beat AC Milan in the 1958 final and Reims again in the final in 1959. Their Argentina-born striker, Alfredo Di Stéfano, was their star player, managing a goal in all four finals.

The final of the 1960 European Cup, played at Hampden Park in Scotland, is remembered as one of the greatest games ever played. Real Madrid, on the verge of five wins in a row, faced German club Eintracht Frankfurt. It began with a surprise goal from the Germans that shocked a record crowd of over 127,000 fans.

The goal stirred Real Madrid into action, and before too long they had hit the post three times. Before half-time they had succeeded in scoring three quick goals. What followed would go down in history and secure Real Madrid's status as the most famous team in football. This was the match that created the legend.

Madrid began the second half with winger Francisco Gento and forward Ferenc Puskás on the rampage. Puskás, a Hungarian with a portly frame, was unstoppable, scoring two quick goals after the break to seal his hat-trick and make it 5–1. A bizarre four-minute spell towards the end of the game saw both teams exchange four goals in as many minutes.

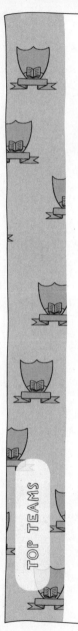

The final score: Real Madrid 7 Eintracht Frankfurt 3. The result established Real Madrid as the model of success, glamour and prestige. It is an image that remains to this day.

THE F⚽TBALL TIMES
SPECIAL EDITION

Real Victory
Real Madrid make Euro history

Real Madrid remain the first and only team to win five successive European Cups. Di Stéfano is the only player to score in five straight finals. And Puskás the only player to score four goals in one final.

BIGGEST RIVALS

Madrid is the biggest city in Spain and the capital. Barcelona is the second biggest city and the capital of the region of Catalonia. The rivalry between Real Madrid and Barcelona is one of the fiercest in football.

QUIZ

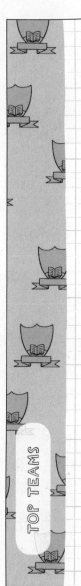

1. **How did American player Alex Morgan celebrate a goal against England in the 2019 World Cup final?**

   a) She shouted in the face of the England goalkeeper.
   b) She did a victory dance.
   c) She ran around the pitch twice.
   d) She pretended to drink a cup of English tea.

2. **What type of energy do Forest Green Rovers use to power their lawnmower?**

   a) Wind
   b) Wave
   c) Solar
   d) Nuclear

3. **What did presenter Gary Lineker wear on TV to celebrate Leicester's title success?**

   a) A Leicester hat and scarf
   b) Just a pair of Leicester underpants
   c) His favourite football boots
   d) Claudio Ranieri's glasses

4. **What record did Liverpool break in winning the 2019–2020 Premier League season?**

   a) Clinching the title with seven games left
   b) Winning every game
   c) Scoring from a throw-in in every game
   d) Their goalkeeper was top scorer

5. **What is the meaning of the Spanish word real in Real Madrid?**

   a) Real
   b) Royal
   c) Radish
   d) Regular

GAME
CHANGERS

A. BELLOS
&
B. LYTTLETON

Dick, Kerr's Ladies

The team that made women's football popular

Today, girls dream of becoming professional players and of winning the World Cup. But things were very different for women a hundred years ago, when football was seen as a sport for men only. Then a women's football team called Dick, Kerr's Ladies changed everything.

In 1914, the First World War began and in the following years several million British men were sent to fight in France. This marked a turning point for women in society. Traditionally, women were expected to stay at home, cook, clean and look after the children. But during the war, with most of the men fighting on the front lines, women took on essential new roles and often worked in factories.

Dick, Kerr and Company, a factory in Lancashire, hired lots of women to help make weapons for the war. One day, in 1917, the male workers challenged the women to a football match.

This was unheard of but as women were doing the same jobs as men, it seemed reasonable that they could join in with football too.

The match was such fun for the women that they decided to carry on playing together. Later that year, they organized a charity football match to raise money for the local hospital that was caring for wounded soldiers. It was a huge success, with about 10,000 spectators and lots of money raised for the hospital.

WONDER WOMAN

Dick, Kerr's Ladies had Lily Parr, the best player of that generation. Parr was famed for her power and aggressive playing style. Her career goal tally stood at more than 900.

Dick, Kerr's Ladies began to play more games, attracting thousands of spectators. Other women's teams started up too. Even when the First World War ended on 11 November 1918, women's football continued to be popular and Dick, Kerr's Ladies became famous as the best team in the country, rarely losing a match. In 1919 when Dick, Kerr's Ladies travelled to play Newcastle United Ladies, the crowd was 35,000! The women quickly became celebrities and inspired other women.

By 1920, Dick, Kerr's Ladies played an average of two games a week for nine months of the year. They played the first women's international match, against France, in front of a crowd of 25,000. In 1921 alone the team played 67 games.

The Football Association, however, were not happy. The men's professional league had restarted in 1919, but the women's games were attracting bigger crowds. At the end of 1921, the FA passed a ruling saying that clubs were not allowed to use their stadiums for women's football, stating that football was "unsuitable for females and ought not to be encouraged". This was a devastating blow, as it left the women's teams with no decent-sized stadiums to play in. Dick, Kerr's Ladies carried on,

but now only a few fans could watch them play. It took until 1971 for the FA to lift its ban on clubs allowing women's football.

Since then, women's football has massively grown in popularity once again, with the 2019 World Cup watched by 1.12 billion viewers.

Jimmy Hill

Campaigner who changed the way we watch football

Jimmy Hill was a footballer, a coach and a well-known TV pundit. His greatest achievements, though, were the new elements he introduced to the game that made football more entertaining for everyone.

Hill died in 2015 but his influence lives on. As head of the Professional Footballers' Association in the 1950s, he successfully campaigned for players to earn their current huge salaries by abolishing the maximum wage, which at the time was £20 per week. Back then, that was the most that the world's best players could earn!

Hill followed that up by launching a succession of innovations that have stood the test of time. His legacy includes these successful changes:

- First electronic scoreboard at matches
- Produced colour-printed matchday programmes
- Created the first panel of football pundits for TV commentary
- Launched slow-motion replays on TV to analyse goals
- Introduced three points for a win to encourage attacking football

Jimmy Hill was a pioneer who loved football. He changed the game and his influence lives on in the way we enjoy football today.

 GOOD SPORT

One of the most memorable moments of Hill's career came in 1972, when he went to watch Arsenal play Liverpool as a fan.

When one of the referee's assistants was injured, the matchday announcer asked if any qualified referees could step in – otherwise the game would have to be abandoned. Hill said yes – even though it meant wearing trainers two sizes too small! Hill could not bear the idea of the match being called off and the fans being disappointed. Pity that the game ended 0–0!

Craig Johnston

Inventor of a futuristic football boot

Growing up in Australia, Craig Johnston wanted to be an architect. He would sketch out different designs for his mum's kitchen and he never lost his passion for finding solutions through design. But he also loved football. He moved across the world for a trial with English club Middlesbrough aged fifteen. Johnston was so determined to succeed that he devised his own training programme to improve his skills. He dribbled around ten bins blindfolded and if he touched one, he would start again. Don't try this at home! He made it into the Middlesbrough first team and, in 1981, he joined Liverpool where he won five league titles as a midfielder. He retired from football aged 27.

Johnston began coaching children and, one rainy day, he was explaining how to swerve a ball. To make a ball swerve, you need to kick it so it spins as it goes forward, which can help get around the wall in a free kick. For the ball to spin, the boot needs to hit the ball at an angle and, during that moment of contact, the boot must rub the ball sideways as much as it can. One of the children said they couldn't do it because the boots were made of leather not table-tennis bats, which were covered in rubber pimples to help the ball swerve. Ping! Pong! Johnston had an idea!

He went home, ripped off the pimply front of a table-tennis bat and attached it to a boot with a rubber band. Immediately, the ball swerved more. Johnston began to design a boot with material that would have more "rub" on the ball than a traditional boot. After three years experimenting with the idea, Johnston declared his invention ready for the game: The Predator was born.

BALL CONTROL

The idea for The Predator was simple: knobbly rubber nodules on the surface of the boot increase friction with the ball and thus improves control.

At first, boot manufacturers rejected him. But Johnston was determined. He asked three of German club Bayern Munich's most famous former players – World Cup winners Franz Beckenbauer, Karl-Heinz Rummenigge and Paul Breitner – to have a kick-around wearing the boots. He filmed them playing and interviewed them talking about the boots afterwards. Johnston couldn't understand what the German players were saying but he showed Adidas the video. The sportswear maker loved it. Adidas didn't have anywhere to test out the boot so they converted an empty swimming pool into a science laboratory and ran experiments to measure The Predator's swerve and accuracy.

Eventually they made The Predator, and players loved the better control and increased power and bend they could generate. David Beckham was wearing Predators when he scored from inside his own half for Manchester United in 1996, as was Zinédine Zidane when he helped France win the 1998 World Cup. Millions of others copied them. The ground-breaking new boot was loved by players of all levels for the way it helped them control the ball.

The Predator boot made Adidas extremely successful and new versions are still manufactured and bought by millions of footballers today – and all thanks to the Australian whose love of design never left him.

FOOTBALL'S BEST INVENTIONS

NAME	DATE	PURPOSE
Goal nets	1891	Ended arguments over whether a goal had been scored
Substitutes	1965	Allowed teams to replace injured players mid-game
Penalty shoot-out	1969	Meant that a winner could be decided if the match was a draw
Red card	1970	Showed players and fans who has been sent off
VAR	2018	Allowed contentious refereeing decisions to be checked using video

Jadon Sancho

England hero showing new path

English winger Jadon Sancho was seventeen when he took a giant step into the unknown. He left his English team, Manchester City, and moved to German club Borussia Dortmund. It was a brave decision: not only did he have to say goodbye to his family and learn a new language, but there was no tradition of players at his level moving to a foreign country at such a young age.

His decision paid off: just over one year later, Sancho was called up to the England squad. He became the first player born this millennium to play for England – well done, Jadon!

Sancho has never been afraid to take risks. On the pitch, he is a tricky winger with mesmerizing ball control, an incredible burst of pace and a fearless attitude.

Off the pitch, it's a similar story: he started out at Watford, but found travelling from his south London home to training three nights a week too exhausting, so he moved to a boarding school nearer Watford. He missed his family and friends. This was the first of many sacrifices he made to get to the top.

Sancho moved to the Manchester City academy when he was fifteen. Two years later, he felt ready to make the step up to play for the first team. At the time, City were building a squad that would win the Premier League, and they were not able to promise that Sancho would play regularly. Sancho just wanted to play!

Borussia Dortmund, one of the most successful clubs in Germany, did make that promise. They convinced Sancho that moving to Dortmund would accelerate his career. They said he would play regularly, receive top coaching and face strong opposition. Sancho went for it.

Dortmund kept their word. Sancho played regularly and improved. He became one of the Bundesliga's best players, at one point scoring in seven successive matches, and earned a regular spot in the England team.

At Dortmund, he found a team that puts faith in young players. In 2020, his team-mates included youthful trio Giovanni Reyna (aged eighteen), Erling Haaland (twenty) and Jude Bellingham (seventeen).

Sancho has now become a role model for young English players keen for an opportunity to play. Rather than waiting on the bench of a Premier League club, they are now prepared to go abroad, challenge themselves with a new language and a new league, listen to a new coach – and play in matches. "If you're willing to make sacrifices anything can happen," Sancho said.

HEY JUDE

The latest young English talent to follow Sancho's footsteps to Germany is Jude Bellingham. A few weeks after turning seventeen, the midfielder left Birmingham City to join Borussia Dortmund. He went straight into the starting line-up and impressed everyone with his quick feet and tactical discipline. After just ten appearances, he received his first call-up to the senior England squad!

Natürlich!

Walter Tull

War hero who challenged the racism of his era

Walter Tull was a gifted footballer and a highly regarded army officer. He was also one of the first Britons with Black heritage to succeed in these professions at a time when racism and prejudice were rife across society.

Tull's father was born in Barbados and his mother was from Kent. Tragically both parents died when Tull was a child and he was sent to live in an orphanage. He had a passion for football and when Tull was 20 he signed for Clapton, an amateur side in London. In his first season, the club won three trophies including the FA Amateur Cup. Tull was snapped up by First Division club Tottenham Hotspur, where he was one of the first people of mixed heritage to play professionally in the UK.

After two years at Spurs, Tull transferred to Northampton Town. He appeared 111 times until, in 1914, the First World War broke out. Britain and France were at war with Germany. The UK government asked Britons to volunteer to fight.

Within months, Tull had enlisted in the army and rose up the ranks to become a second lieutenant. He was one of the first people of Black heritage to join the officer class in the regular British Army, at a time when regulations made this almost impossible.

STANDING UP TO RACISM

During his football career Walter Tull faced terrible prejudice and discrimination. For example, when Spurs played Bristol City, a newspaper reported that a section of the crowd shouted abuse at Tull. The article said: "Let me tell those Bristol hooligans that Tull is so clean in mind and method as to be a model for all white men who play football."

In 1917, when Tull was serving in Italy, he led 26 men on a night raid against an enemy position. All his men returned unharmed despite coming under heavy fire. His seniors commended him for his "gallantry and coolness".

In March 1918, a few months before the end of the war, Tull was stationed in northern France. Germany unleashed a fierce attack on the British front line, firing more than 3.5 million shells. The casualties were horrific: Tull was one of about half a million soldiers who died. He was 29 years old.

On the pitch Tull had shown great courage in getting on with his job when faced with racist abuse, and even greater bravery with his men during the war.

Walter Tull was a hero three times over: on the pitch, on the battlefield and in life. He has been commemorated in Northampton, his former club town, where there is a statue in his honour. On the 100th anniversary of his death, politicians supported an ongoing campaign for Tull to be awarded the Military Cross for his exceptional wartime effort.

Walter Tull was a member of the Football Battalion, a group of several hundred professional and amateur footballers who fought in the First World War.

QUIZ

1. **What reason did the Football Association give for banning women's football in 1921?**

   a) They didn't want the women to get too tired.
   b) They said it was unsuitable for females.
   c) They thought it was boring.
   d) They wanted women to go back to work in the factories.

2. **Which of these changes did Jimmy Hill introduce to football?**

   a) He made snacks available to buy at the stadium.
   b) He allowed all players to touch the ball with their hands.
   c) He raised the salary for referees.
   d) He launched the first electronic scoreboard at matches.

3. **What piece of sporting equipment inspired Craig Johnston to make The Predator boot?**

   a) Table-tennis bat
   b) Tennis racquet
   c) Baseball bat
   d) Hockey stick

4. **What record does Jadon Sancho hold?**

   a) Youngest England player
   b) First England player to play in Germany
   c) First player born in the 21st century to play for England
   d) Fastest England player ever

5. **What was Walter Tull commended for by his superiors in the army?**

   a) His fantastic football skills
   b) His neat uniform
   c) His gallantry and coolness
   d) His delicious cooking

FOOTBALL SCHOOL LIBRARY

WBD SPECIAL

Unbelievable Tales

A. BELLOS & B. LYTTLETON

The Boy Who Would Not Grow

Lionel Messi, the Argentina forward, is undoubtedly one of the best players in the history of the game. But Messi almost never made it to the top. When he was younger, he had a medical condition that stopped him from growing and meant he might be too short to become a professional player.

Messi grew up in Rosario, a city in Argentina, and joined local team Newell's Old Boys when he was just six years old. His youth team became near invincible, but by the time he was ten, all his team-mates were growing taller  much faster than he was. As a result, he suffered at the hands of bullies who were mean about his height.

Eventually Messi was diagnosed with a rare growth hormone disorder. Hormones are chemicals produced by our bodies that control how our bodies and emotions work. Messi's pituitary gland, a pea-sized organ in the brain responsible for the balance of hormones, was not sending out the right amount of growth hormone. As well as stopping growth, a lack of this hormone can lead to poor vision and lower immunity. These issues could have held back Messi's career.

The doctor prescribed Messi with a three-year course of treatment which was expensive, costing around $1,000 per month. It was a tough time. "Every night I had to stick a needle into my legs, night after night after night, every day of the week, and this over a period of three years," he said. In the middle of his course of treatment Messi's family was no longer able to pay for it. Newell's could not afford it and nor could River Plate, another club who were interested in Messi. Only one team was prepared to sign Messi and take on the costs of the treatment for another year. That club was Barcelona.

So, aged just thirteen, he moved to Spain with his father to start his career with Barcelona. Luckily the treatment worked and Messi began to grow.

Messi is now 1.70 metres (5ft 6ins), which is a normal adult height, if a bit shorter than average. Yet his short stature is now an advantage, since it allows him to be more agile than other playe

Short people make better dribblers than tall people because short people have shorter, lighter limbs. This means they find it easier to control their balance when running with the ball

 A TALL STORY

Goalkeepers are often tall. Taller people have been shown by scientists to be better at judging distances, possibly because they are used to looking at the ground from further away.

than tall people do. Small players also spend less energy on maintaining stability because they don't have to move large heavy bones around, which means they can spend more energy on running, speeding up and controlling the ball.

Messi has made Barcelona the greatest team of his generation. He has won ten league titles, four Champions Leagues and three Club World Cup titles with Barcelona; and he has won the Ballon D'Or award for the world's best player five times. If you put all his trophies on top of each other, they would be taller than him!

The Footballers Who Pooed on the Pitch

Footballers have to think carefully about when they go to the loo. No one wants to be caught out in the middle of a game, as you can't rush to the toilet with 50,000 fans watching you. But sometimes it does happen – even to football's biggest stars!

Planning a poo is all about timing. In order to perfectly time a poo you need to plan when you eat. Clubs make sure their players eat a meal three hours before a game. This allows plenty of time for the food to pass through the digestive system. The digestive system is the part of the body that takes in food, breaks it down, absorbs the nutrients and, last but not least, makes poo.

The journey of a poo starts when food enters the mouth. After it's been chewed, the mashed-up food plummets down a long tube, called the oesophagus, to the stomach. There it is churned around and chemicals in the stomach break down the food, with the help of other organs such as the liver and pancreas. The final stage takes place in the small and large intestines, where the nutrients are absorbed into the blood and what remains is expelled through your rectum and anus (the bum) as poo.

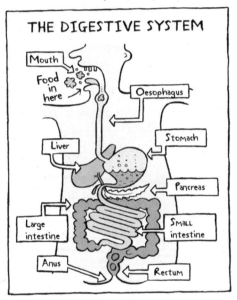

THE DIGESTIVE SYSTEM

Mouth
Food in here →
Oesophagus
Liver
Stomach
Pancreas
Large intestine
Small intestine
Anus
Rectum

Just before kick-off, every player on the team will go for a poo so they are playing on an empty stomach. But players can still get their timings wrong and be left flushed with something other than pride during a match. Let's meet three footballers who have all had toilet trouble!

A messy business

Gary Lineker was one of England's best ever strikers. At the 1986 World Cup, he scored six goals and won the prize, known as the Golden Boot, for top scorer. But the 1990 World Cup started quite, well, poo-rly for him. "I tried to tackle someone, stretched and relaxed myself and erm..." Lineker said of the moment he pooed himself on the pitch against the Republic of Ireland in England's first game of the tournament. "I was not very well, I was poorly at half-time. I was very fortunate that it rained that night so I could do something about it, but it was messy. You can see myself rubbing the ground like a dog trying to clean it. It was the most horrendous experience of my life." There was some good news: the Irish players did not want to get too close to him. "I have never found so much space after that in my life," he laughed.

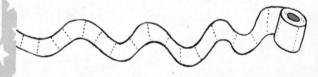

Caught short

In 2011, Mexico were drawing 1–1 with local rivals USA. There were just a few minutes left to play when Mexico midfielder Omar Arellano bent down to adjust his socks. As the TV cameras panned in for a close-up, there was a surprise for viewers: a suspicious-looking brown stain on the back of his white shorts, which was aired around the world.

Dier straits

England midfielder Eric Dier ran off the pitch in the middle of the match when his Tottenham Hotspur team were losing 1–0 to Chelsea in a cup tie in 2020. He was desperate for the loo and nothing was going to stop him going! The team's situation improved when he got back on the pitch. Spurs went on to win the game, thanks in part to Dier scoring a penalty. Dier was named man of the match – not bad considering his case of Dier-rea!

The GOAT Mascot

For many fans, a football team's mascot is a beloved symbol of their club that brings them good luck. One German club, Cologne, can claim to have the mascot who is literally the Greatest Of All Time … because he is a goat!

Cologne's mascot is called Hennes and he is a billy goat, which is the name for a male goat. (Females are called nanny goats.) It is said that the tradition started in 1950, when a circus owner gave a billy goat to the club as a lucky charm. They named him after Hennes Weisweiler, who was Cologne coach at the time.

Goats only have a lifespan of about fifteen years, so when Hennes died he was replaced by Hennes II, and so on until Hennes IX became the mascot in 2019. The Hennes tradition has become so popular with fans

YOU'RE KIDDING

Scientists say that some goats' accents change to fit their surroundings when they move away from their family.

Bâaâaâa

Bêêêêê

that he is now on their club badge, and Cologne are known in Germany as the Billy Goats.

The most famous of Cologne's goats was Hennes VII. He appeared in TV shows, including once as a murder victim in a German crime drama! Hennes IX has his own social media channels so when he isn't at matches, fans can stay up-to-date with his life at Cologne Zoo. Let's hope he doesn't post anything too gruff!

The Mystery of the Stolen World Cup

The original World Cup trophy, given to the winners of the World Cup from 1930 to 1970, has one of the most baffling histories in football. It was the centre of THREE separate mysteries and still to this day has not been found.

Let's open the casebook for the stolen World Cup and see if you can succeed where the world's best sleuths have failed.

 TRIUMPHANT TROPHIES

Trophies have been part of sporting events for thousands of years. In the ancient Olympic Games, the world's earliest major sporting tournament held from around 800 BC, victorious athletes were crowned with a wreath of olive leaves cut from a sacred tree. Nowadays, trophies are usually made out of metal and, in the case of football, often shaped like a cup.

Mystery I:
The Rimet Riddle

Frenchman Jules Rimet planned the first
World Cup in 1930. He asked Abel Lafleur, a
sculptor from Paris, to design the trophy for the
competition. Lafleur made a silver trophy of a
cup being supported by Nike, the Greek goddess
of victory, and coated it with gold. It was later
renamed the Jules Rimet trophy. Experts believe
something happened to the Jules Rimet trophy
between 1954 and 1958. The trophy Brazil won in
Sweden at the1958 World Cup looked different
to the one that West Germany won in 1954. The
1958 version appeared to be 5 centimetres taller
and had a different base.

MYSTERY: Was the 1958 trophy
a copy? If so,
where is the
original?

STATUS:

UNSOLVED

Mystery 2:
Stolen on a Sunday

In 1966, England hosted the World Cup. The Jules Rimet trophy was on display in a central London museum for a few months before the tournament began. One Sunday, when the guards were not looking, a thief or thieves broke in through the back doors and stole the trophy. It was a huge embarrassment for English football and Scotland Yard was called in to solve the crime.

MYSTERY: Where was the trophy?

STATUS: A dog called Pickles found it seven days later, wrapped in newspaper under a bush in south London.

SOLVED

MYSTERY: Who was behind the theft?

STATUS:

UNSOLVED

Mystery 3:
Burglary in Brazil

FIFA had a rule that the first country to win the World Cup three times would be allowed to keep the trophy. When Brazil won their third title in 1970, the Brazilians took the Jules Rimet trophy home. In 1983, it was stolen from the third floor of the Brazilian Football Confederation office in Rio de Janeiro. No one has seen it since. Brazil's investigators said it had been melted down into gold bars, but this can't be right, since the original trophy wasn't made of gold!

MYSTERY: Where is the trophy?

STATUS: UNSOLVED

After 1970, FIFA had a new trophy made. This time it was made of gold and featured two human figures holding up a globe. So far, this trophy hasn't gone missing. Whoever gets to the bottom of either of the three unsolved mysteries above would be a true world champion, a soccer Sherlock Holmes. If you have any ideas, please let us know!

The Thai Cave Rescue

Can you imagine what it would be like to spend weeks trapped underground in the dark with no way to contact your family or friends? Well, this is exactly what happened to the Wild Boars football team and their coach Ake, who were rescued after spending seventeen days without food or light in the Tham Luang cave in northern Thailand. The daring rescue attempt, led by elite Navy SEALs and international diving experts, took three days and gripped millions around the world.

The dramatic story began after football practice one Saturday in June 2018, when the group cycled to the network of long narrow tunnels and chambers that are a popular local tourist destination. They left their bikes at the cave's entrance and took off their football boots. They had all been to the cave before, so took with them only their torches, some water and a few snacks.

After an hour's exploring, the Wild Boars realized that the cave chamber they were in was quickly filling up with water and there was no way out. They escaped from the rising water to a dry, sandy spot and sat down to spend the night inside the cave. At first, their coach wasn't too worried. He thought that they would be rescued in the morning. He made the boys huddle together to stay warm. But no one came the next day, or the day after that. Soon the group lost all track of time and once their torch batteries ran out, they were left in complete darkness. It was cold and they had to lick the walls of the cave for water. Everyone felt faint and tired. A week passed and the boys were still trapped with nothing to eat.

Inside the cave, the boys had no idea that they had become the most famous football team in the world. Their parents had rushed to the cave when they didn't return home, found their bikes and boots and raised the alarm. The race to find the Wild Boars was quickly followed by TV stations, news websites and newspapers, first in Thailand and then across the globe. No one knew if the boys were alive or dead.

The rescue operation began the day after the boys went missing. The challenge was to work out where the boys might be in the cave network. Thai Navy SEALs faced freezing cold water, strong currents and narrow tunnels and, of course, it was pitch black. Expert cave divers from other countries also offered their help. By the tenth day, many people had lost hope that the Wild Boars would be found alive. Then two British divers popped out of the water in a chamber more than a mile underground. Their torches lit up thirteen skinny people wearing football kit, sitting in the dark. Against the odds, Ake and the boys were miraculously all still alive.

However, it was going to be very risky to get the team out safely. Even the experienced divers had found the tunnels difficult to swim through. Divers brought the boys food and clothes while they worked out a plan.

The operation began a week later. Each boy was given an oxygen mask and strapped to a stretcher, which was guided by a diver. The operation involved 100 people and took three days. Everyone was overjoyed to see the Wild Boars re-emerge from darkness after their seventeen-day ordeal. "This experience taught me to value my life," said one of the boys afterwards. "This event has made me stronger."

QUIZ

1. **Which Argentinian club did Lionel Messi join aged six before he moved to Barcelona?**

   a) River Plate
   b) Rosario Central
   c) Newell's Old Boys
   d) Boca Juniors

2. **How long before a game should footballers eat a meal in order to best time a poo?**

   a) Three hours
   b) Fifteen minutes
   c) Five hours
   d) One day

3. **What is a female goat called?**

   a) Mummy goat
   b) Sister goat
   c) Granny goat
   d) Nanny goat

4. **What was the name of the dog who found the Jules Rimet Cup in 1966?**

   a) Dill
   b) Cucumber
   c) Pickles
   d) Spot

5. **Where were Thai football team, the Wild Boars, trapped for seventeen days?**

   a) An underground cave
   b) Their football stadium
   c) A supermarket
   d) Their coach's house

QUIZ ANSWERS

FANTASTIC
FOOTBALLERS

1. d)

2. b)

3. b)

4. c)

5. a)

GAME
CHANGERS

1. b)

2. d)

3. a)

4. c)

5. c)

TOP
TEAMS

1. d)

2. c)

3. b)

4. a)

5. b)

UNBELIEVABLE
TALES

1. c)

2. a)

3. d)

4. c)

5. a)

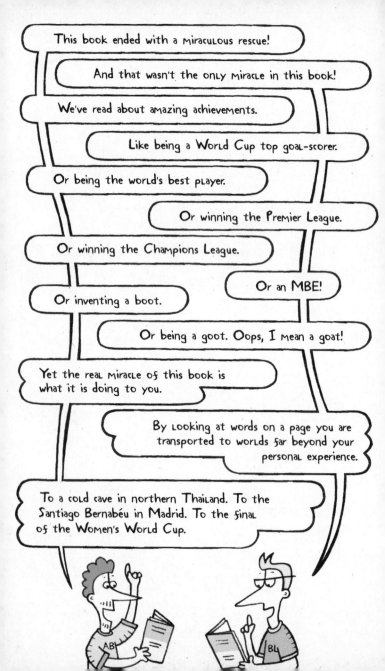

Yes, it's the miracle of reading!
Reading is one of the most enjoyable things to do in life.
It is also one of the most useful.
Reading fires up your imagination and creativity, you get to find out new stuff, and, let's not forget, you get to laugh at jokes about poo.
Keep on reading everyone! We don't even mind if you read books written by people other than us!
I hope we're all on the same page with that!
Alex, we are literally on the same page!
Ha ha ha and see you all soon!
AB
BL

WORLD BOOK DAY

On your bookmarks, get set, read!

Well hello there! We are

Overjoyed that you have joined our celebration of

Reading books and sharing stories, because we

Love bringing books to you.

Did you know, we are a charity dedicated to celebrating the

Brilliance of reading for pleasure for everyone, everywhere?

Our mission is to help you discover brand new stories and

Open your mind to exciting worlds and characters, from

Kings and queens to wizards and pirates to animals and adventurers and so many more. We couldn't

Do it without all the amazing authors and illustrators, booksellers and bookshops, publishers, schools and libraries out there –

And most importantly, we couldn't do it all without . . .

You!

Changing lives through a love of books and shared reading.

World Book Day is a registered charity funded by publishers and booksellers in the UK & Ireland.

ILLUSTRATOR *Rob Biddulph*

SPONSORED BY

From breakfast to bedtime, there's always time to discover and share stories together. You can . . .

1 Take a trip to your local bookshop

Brimming with brilliant books and helpful booksellers to share awesome reading recommendations, you can also enjoy booky events with your favourite authors and illustrators.

Find your local bookshop:
booksellers.org.uk/bookshopsearch

2 Join your local library

That wonderful place where the hugest selection of books you could ever want to read awaits – and you can borrow them for FREE! Plus expert advice and fantastic free family reading events.

Find your local library:
gov.uk/local-library-services/

3 Check out the World Book Day website

Looking for reading tips, advice and inspiration? There is so much to discover at **worldbookday.com**, packed with fun activities, audiobooks, videos, competitions and all the latest book news galore.

MORE FROM FOOTBALL SCHOOL

Find out about our amazing world through football

"We love this book series!"
Match of the Day Weekly

"Hilarious ... packed with amazing football facts, cartoons, jokes..."
The Week Junior

"Intelligent, inspiring, funny..."
Head of Education, Premier League

Discover incredible true stories about top players and teams

Coming soon

Test your football knowledge and laugh out loud

Coming soon